ISSUES IN SPORTS

HIGH-PRESSURE YOUTH SPORTS

BY MARYANN HUDSON

Published by ABDO Publishing Company, PO Box 398166, Minneapolis, MN 55439.

Printed in the United States of America,
North Mankato, Minnesota
102013
012014

THIS BOOK CONTAINS AT LEAST 10% RECYCLED MATERIALS.

Editor: Chrös McDougall
Series Designer: Craig Hinton

Photo credits: Shutterstock Images, cover, 1; ESPN/AP Images, 5; AP Images, 6, 29; BananaStock/Thinkstock, 11, 17; Jeff Janowski/Wilmington Star-News/AP Images, 13; David J. Phillip/AP Images, 15; Tom E. Puskar/AP Images, 18; Gene J. Puskar/AP Images, 21; Ryan Soderlin/Casper Star-Tribune/AP Images, 24; Jeffrey Thompson/Minnesota Public Radio/AP Images, 26; Martha Irvine/AP Images, 31; Thinkstock, 32, 41, 55; Phelan M. Ebenhack/AP Images, 35; Armando Franca/AP Images, 37; Beth A. Keiser/AP Images, 45; Andy Colwell/The Patriot-News/AP Images, 47; David Duprey/AP Images, 50; Paul Sancya/AP Images, 56; The Birmingham News, Mark Almond/AP Images, 59

Library of Congress Control Number: 2013946563

Cataloging-in-Publication Data

Hudson, Maryann.
High-pressure youth sports / Maryann Hudson.
p. cm. -- (Issues in sports)
Includes bibliographical references and index.
ISBN 978-1-62403-122-9
1. Sports for children--Social aspects--Juvenile literature. 2. Sports for children--Moral and ethical aspects--Juvenile literature. I. Title.
796.083--dc23

2013946563

Content Consultant:
Rick Howard
Founding Member and Immediate Past-Chair of the NSCA Youth Special Interest Group

TABLE OF CONTENTS

CHAPTER 1

Screen grabs show Rutgers men's basketball coach Mike Rice physically abusing his players during a practice.

WHERE DID THE FUN GO?

Rutgers University men's basketball coach Mike Rice was totally out of control. He shoved and pushed his players. He cursed at them. He even threw balls at the players. Some coaches use aggressive tactics to motivate players. But this went over the line.

An assistant coach had secretly filmed the incident. The video went viral. Fans had seen Rice screaming and grabbing at his players during games. They had never seen anything like this, though. The video was on its way to getting 2.1 million views.

Yelling and grabbing at people is not accepted on the streets. The public often accepts when coaches do this, though. It is a coach's job

Indiana University men's basketball coach Bobby Knight throws a chair across the court in frustration during a 1985 game.

to motivate his or her players. Some say screaming at and insulting the players is one way to motivate them. And fiery coaches have certainly had success. College basketball coach Bobby Knight yelled and screamed at his players for 42 seasons. He retired in 2008 with more wins than any coach in Division I history. However, there is a line between fiery and dangerous. Rice was physically and verbally abusing his players. The public showed little sympathy to him for this behavior.

At first, the university stood by Rice. But the public was outraged. So Rutgers fired Rice on April 3, 2013. The school's athletic director later resigned over his handling of the situation as well.

Not all coaches have such aggressive styles. But coaches who do use aggressive coaching tactics are increasingly coming under question. Many youth players say an aggressive coaching style does not make them feel confident. And there is some debate as to whether it makes them play better. In addition, some medical professionals believe this behavior can

SPORTS AS CHILD ABUSE?

Fred Engh is the founder and president of the National Alliance for Youth Sports (NAYS). His organization provides training for coaches nationwide. Several years ago, Engh said he heard a shocking statement while attending a conference. A doctor speaking there called youth sports the greatest form of legalized child abuse in the United States. At first Engh said he was stunned. Then he decided it was true. "Just take a moment and look around the next time you're at a youth sports event," Engh wrote. "The negative words and actions of many coaches on the field and parents in the stands are truly shocking."

cause real harm to kids. They call aggressive coaching behavior emotional abuse. The medical professionals warn it can cause long-term self-worth problems for kids.

LOSING THE FUN

Approximately 44 million kids ages 6 to 18 participate in sports in the United States. What troubles health professionals is that so many quit. Approximately 70 percent of children quit sports by age 13, according to a study by Michigan State University. And the number one reason they give for quitting is that they are not having any fun. Yet numerous studies have shown that fun is the main reason why kids play sports to begin with.

Sports can enrich a child's life both mentally and physically. They can teach skills such as teamwork, responsibility, cooperation, hard work, and discipline. Sports can also teach kids how to handle success and failure. But sometimes a sports experience can get ruined for a child.

Frequent games and practices can take a toll on the body. This is especially true for athletes who specialize in one sport. Young athletes can suffer a mental toll, too. Some kids are constantly running to and from practices and games. They might not have time to take a break and relax. This can all lead to overuse injuries or burnout. Other times, an overly aggressive coach can ruin the experience. Extreme pressure from parents or from within oneself can also take the fun out of sports. And in extreme cases, issues such as sexual abuse from coaches or teammates can have a lifelong effect.

MAKING CHANGES

Youth sports are growing. Issues and pressures are adding up. But experts are working on ways to counter these negative aspects. They want youth sports to be as positive an experience for kids as possible.

The United States Olympic Committee (USOC) oversees the national governing bodies (NGBs) for many popular sports in the United States, such as basketball and soccer. This oversight involves picking the US Olympic Team. But the USOC and the NGBs are also involved with youth sports. The USOC created a program and Web site called SafeSport (www.safesport.org). The program was designed to help stop six bad behaviors in sports: bullying, hazing, and harassment, plus physical, sexual, and emotional misconduct. The program's Web site has guidelines to help athletes, coaches, and parents recognize and report abuse in sports. Health professionals say that physical abuse is not just pushing and shoving. Physical abuse also includes things such as requiring an athlete to play hurt and not allowing an athlete to get proper rest, nutrition, and hydration.

Safe Kids Worldwide is an organization that works to protect kids from sports injuries. It has created several guidelines for sports safety.

FITNESS HELPS IN SCHOOL

Sports and other physical activities are good for one's health. Physical fitness can also affect kids' performance in school, studies have found. The American College of Sports Medicine (ACSM) published one of those studies. The ACSM tested 338 sixth-grade students at a school in central Illinois. Students underwent tests to determine their body mass index (BMI) and their ability to perform pull-ups. The researchers found that kids who were more fit tended to do better on standardized tests.

Sports can lose their appeal when the pressure or time commitment become too much for young athletes.

The guidelines include even simple things such as how many glasses of water an athlete should drink during play. In addition, some states and sports organizations have guidelines for playing when it is very hot outside. And equipment manufacturers strive to produce safer products.

Organizations such as the NAYS and the Positive Coaching Alliance (PCA) train and regulate volunteer coaches and administrators nationwide. They emphasize the strict principles of safety and fun.

After all, that is what the majority of kids want the most from sports—they want to have some fun.

THE NUMBERS

One survey tested 300 kids from ages 8 to 14 who play team sports. Of those kids, 84 percent said they wished they had more fun playing. Nearly one-third of the kids said they wished adults did not watch their games. The 2012 study was done by i9 Sports in Tampa, Florida. The kids in the survey said adults yell too much and are too distracting, making players nervous. The kids also said adults put unnecessary pressure on them to play better and win. Eighty-four percent said they have quit a team or wanted to. Forty-seven percent said playing was not any fun.

CHAPTER 2

An injured soccer player is helped off the field by a teammate and a coach.

OVERUSED AND OVERDONE

Many kids thrive on the competition in sports. They want to get better and better. That attitude can be motivating. But it can also be exhausting.

In the 1980s and 1990s, travel teams began turning youth sports upside down. These teams had been around for a while. But suddenly they became hugely popular for children and their families. Players would spend hours traveling to other cities or states to compete.

Travel teams are sometimes called elite, select, or other names. They are generally more competitive and selective than recreational leagues or house leagues. The athletes usually have to make the teams through

CFSC
CAPE FEAR
adidas

tryouts. And once the season starts, teams practice or play games several days a week. Similar commitments exist in top-level individual sports.

These commitments also affect entire families. Parents must spend many hours each week taking their kids to and from sports commitments. In addition, traveling can be expensive. Sometimes families have to stay overnight or eat out. But many see this commitment as a worthwhile investment. These kids want to take a serious approach to their sports. They want to be the best they can be. So more and more kids are signing up for travel teams or other serious training plans.

There are risks involved with serious training. In the past it was common for kids to play several sports each year. But the rise of travel teams has led to mass specialization for youths under 14. These kids pick one sport and commit to it. That often means the athlete plays year-round. Sometimes athletes play for multiple teams each year, too. This is common in sports such as basketball and soccer. Some people believe this commitment is necessary. However, experts believe it can be harmful.

STARTING YOUNG

Travel team leagues start for children at a young age. One T-ball travel team in Texas was organized for five- and six-year-olds. Children as young as eight play travel hockey and soccer. Practices are held twice a week or more. Games are played on the weekends and weeknights. Leagues are available year-round, providing players with more skill development.

OVERUSE INJURIES

Travel teams provide many benefits for young athletes. But some medical professionals say that the year-round schedule can also cause children

Elite US gymnasts stretch together at a national team training camp.

harm. Each year, US children under 14 suffer approximately 3.5 million sports injuries. Some of those injuries are called acute. These include injuries such as broken arms and legs. But half of the injuries are classified as overuse injuries. These injuries occur when the body rebels and breaks down from continued use of the same body parts.

Athletes who specialize in one sport tend to do the same motions over and over. This can cause parts of the body to become swollen, strained, and fatigued. These injuries can happen over time. They can

RESTING SKILLS

Safe Kids Worldwide believes young athletes need to focus on sport skills. The organization also believes kids need to learn resting skills. It issued guidelines to ensure healthy participation in sports. One suggestion was that athletes take at least two to three months away from a specific sport each year. The organization states athletes should have at least one to two days off each week from organized physical activity. And the intensity of training should not increase by more than 10 percent each week. So an athlete who does 10 reps of training one week should do no more than 11 the next week. Safe Kids Worldwide also encourages athletes to play on only one team per season.

also happen when an athlete increases the intensity of training too quickly. Experts say fitness and skill development must be balanced to avoid overtraining. That is true whether an athlete is competing in one sport or multiple sports. In general, experts advise that children train no more than 18 to 20 hours a week. Without time to rest and heal, minor tweaks and weak limbs can develop into overuse injuries.

Tony Pena is a high school-certified athletic trainer in California. He said overuse injuries are the most common injuries he treats.

"I do treat acute injuries, but most of what I treat is overuse, and it's not just from specialization," Pena said. "Kids play football, then later in the day they have basketball. Then some play volleyball. Then they have club volleyball. It's just too much. The body needs time to repair and recover."

Stress fractures and tendinitis are examples of overuse injuries. Stress fractures happen when someone strains his or her bones repeatedly. The bone breaks down faster than it can build up. The result is a small break

Athletes who spend too much time participating in one sport are more likely to suffer from overuse injuries or burnout.

in a bone. Tendinitis occurs when muscles cannot keep up with the same routine. Eventually the tendons inflame and become painful to use.

Overuse injuries can happen in any sport. They often occur in the knees, heels, necks, elbows, and shoulders. Doctors say overuse injuries have increased dramatically during the past decade. They now see injuries in children they had previously seen only in adults.

National Football League (NFL) commissioner Roger Goodell visits a 2013 youth football clinic designed to promote player safety.

Overuse injuries and overtraining can also affect an athlete's mind and heart. Some athletes invest a lot of time, effort, and money into a sport. It can be devastating for them to be stuck on the sideline with an injury.

OVERUSE IS PREVENTABLE

Doctors' frustration with overuse injuries is that they are preventable. The easiest way to prevent these injuries is by simply backing off training and letting the body recover. Athletes should also avoid drastic increases in training intensity.

Overuse injuries can also be prevented with strength training and conditioning, doctors say. Strength training is for increasing muscle strength and endurance. The Mayo Clinic advises that children as young as seven or eight years old can do strength training as part of an overall fitness plan. The key is that kids that age have careful supervision. Heavy weights and poor form can put too much strain on young muscles. So kids that age should not strength train in an attempt to bulk up. Strength training at that age is mostly to improve endurance and help protect the body from injury.

START LATER, FOCUS WIDE

Athletic skills such as jumping, mental focus, speed, and balance are different depending on the sport. But experts say developing a wide range of skills can make a child an overall better athlete. Focusing on one sport denies a young athlete the chance to develop skills in other sports. Research also shows no benefit to future sports performance by starting a child at age four or sooner. Starting this young might lead to injuries and burnout, says Paul Stricker. He is a sports medicine pediatrician and former US Olympic Team physician. "Motor skills such as balance and running don't fully develop until age six or seven, while the ability to visually track moving objects doesn't mature until age eight or nine," he said.

CHAPTER 3

Parents cheer on their sons at the 2012 Little League World Series in South Williamsport, Pennsylvania.

PARENTAL PRESSURE

Parents can be a young athlete's greatest supporter. Parents can also be a major distraction.

A 2010 survey compared parental behavior at youth sporting events around the world. It asked adults if they had seen parents become verbally or physically abusive toward youth coaches and officials. In the United States, 60 percent of those surveyed said they had witnessed this. India was second highest at 59 percent. Italy (55 percent), Argentina (54), Canada (53), and Australia (50) rounded out the top six. Australians call this problem "The Ugly Parent Syndrome."

RIKE OUT
HOME
0
KIER BaBy!
Go NE 15
NE
New England
New England
VIP
New England
2012
LITTLE LEAGUE
BASEBALL

The majority of parents are not abusive to their child athletes. When parents do act up at sporting events, however, the incidents range in severity. Sometimes it is a simple shout of disgust at a referee's call or a rough play. On rare occasions, the incidents can be extreme. One extreme example happened in Vallejo, California. A parent fired gunshots into an opposing parent's car after a T-ball game.

Cases of extreme violence have increased but are not common. But it is common to see parents shouting from the stands or the sidelines. Kids hear it, and they see it. *Sports Illustrated Kids* reported that 74 percent of its young readers have seen out-of-control adults at their games.

There are different reasons why parents get emotional at their kids' sporting events. One study questioned 340 parents after watching their children's soccer games. Fifty-three percent of the parents said they were angry at some point in the match. The parents gave several reasons for their anger. The most frequent were situations with referees, their own child, and their child's team. However, grandparents have been found to be calmer at

THE PROWLER

Bob Bigelow is a former National Basketball Association (NBA) player. He also lectures on parenting and has written about parental involvement in youth sports. In one of his books, Bigelow described the typical overbearing parent. "In this world of high volume and hyperventilating, one parent stands out. You can hear him from the parking lot. 'Mark your man,' he screams to his little boy. Red-faced and nearly breathless, this father runs up and down the sidelines, keeping pace with every play. 'See the ball,' he growls. And this, his favorite one-liner from the General Patton Does Soccer playbook: 'Stay within yourself.'" Bigelow goes on to write about when the other team scores. The father asks his son why he is not listening. The son answers: "I'm listening dad, but I don't know what you're talking about."

youth sporting events. They tend to be happy just to sit and watch the games. For this reason, some kids say they enjoy having grandparents at their games.

NAYS founder and president Fred Engh said some parents undergo a great change in emotions when they arrive at their kids' sporting event. They get competitive. Sometimes they want their kids to win even more than the kids do.

"These parents are loud, negative, and disruptive, a terrible influence to every child playing the game," Engh said.

The parents' actions can have negative effects on the kids, Engh said. "[The parents] have failed to recognize that many of the things that they do to children in the name of sports can actually be considered child abuse," he said.

OVER-INVOLVED PARENTS

Frank Smoll is a professor at the University of Washington. He believes over-involved parents are one of the biggest problems in youth sports. Smoll says parents live through their children to relive their own youth. But parents do not know when to stop, he said. Instead, they push and push.

"It can be very difficult [for a parent] to recognize when you're in it," Smoll said. "They are in a state of . . . denial."

A mother cheers for her son's team during a high school basketball game.

Parents can teach children a lot about handling disappointment and success. For example, a parent's positive feedback can teach children how to feel good about themselves. But children can also become confused when parents become too involved in their children's sports. These children might wonder why they are playing the sport, and for whom. They might think the activity means more to the parent. Sometimes a parent's and a child's expectations might be different. A parent might expect a child to perform higher than the child is capable of. Or sometimes the parent pushes a child to participate at a level the child is not interested in.

Al Rosen is a former Major League Baseball (MLB) player. Playing poorly and losing are realities for athletes at all levels. Rosen said one of the worst things parents can do is to withdraw attention, love, or affection when their children struggle in sports.

"[Children] quickly realize they are no longer competing to win the match, but rather to win the love and approval of their parents," Rosen said.

BURNING OUT

Many kids thrive on the competition in sports. They want to get better and better. That attitude can be motivating. But sometimes well-meaning parents can turn that motivation into burnout.

Sports psychologists define burnout as physical and emotional exhaustion of an athlete. This leads to a lack of caring about the sport. Burnout can be caused by different factors. Some athletes feel trapped by the constant pressure to win

TRY IT ALONE

Being part of a team can help children develop self-esteem. But some kids do not do well as part of a team, according to Susan Stiffelman. She is a parent, coach, and family therapist. Stiffelman suggests that kids who do poorly in big groups should try individual sports such as golf or tennis. Less competitive activities could be a good option, too. Stiffelman said children with a very sensitive nature sometimes dislike team sports. The pressure they feel from other players and the coach becomes a burden. "While it's fine for kids to stretch out of their comfort zone, if a sensitive child is paralyzed with anxiety because of what is or should be an enjoyable activity, I would look for an alternative." she said.

Parents react to a penalty during a youth hockey game.

and perform. They no longer feel a sense of reward or enjoyment from playing. Youth athletes also put a lot of time and energy into a sport. They might feel overwhelmed. Committed athletes sometimes feel like they are missing out on life outside of organized sports.

Pressure can come from many different areas. Most athletes want to improve and be successful. They also want to perform well for their teammates and coaches. But sometimes coaches or teammates put too much pressure on an athlete. The athlete might feel like he or she is always straining to reach other people's expectations.

Some athletes simply become overcommitted. They sign up for teams or sports that involve too much time. These athletes are constantly shuffling between games or practices. This takes time away from schoolwork. It also limits an athlete's free time to hang out with friends. But there is great pressure to keep up the routine. To remain on the team, the athlete has to find a way to make it all work.

Yet quitting a sport can also be tough on kids, too. Sometimes kids no longer want to continue playing. But they feel they are letting down their parents, coaches, and teammates by quitting. They also might fear being labeled a quitter by their peers.

"Often, we give a conditional label to kids who finally decide they really don't want to do this," said Dr. Thomas Tutko, a psychology professor and author. "We call them quitters. So the children may not have fun *and* they're also labeled as quitters, [a great] insult. Basically what you're saying is that they're not worthwhile."

THE PARENTS' ROLE IN BURNOUT

Well-meaning parents sometimes miss the warning signs of burnout. They want to give their children every possible opportunity to do well in life. In sports, that might mean signing up for several sports teams. That can mean a game or a practice every night. Or parents might let kids specialize in one sport. The kids play year-round. These kids might even

STRAIGHT TO THE SOURCE

Scars of the Heart

New York Yankees outfielder Mickey Mantle was one of baseball's biggest stars in the 1950s and 1960s. Yet the Hall of Famer once announced on a television talk show that he wet the bed until he was 16 years old. Mantle's wife, Merlyn, said the bedwetting was a result of pressure. Mantle's father pressured young Mickey to play baseball. And Mantle put great pressure on himself to be one of the best. Merlyn wrote:

> *I would hope that this would not be taken as demeaning him. But it is important, I think, in understanding what he went through, and how much he wanted to please his dad. This is what the pressure of wanting that approval did to him. He told me that he knew from the time he was five years old that he wanted to be a ballplayer and he could never face his father if he didn't make it to the major leagues.*

Source: Merlyn Mantle. A Hero All His Life. *New York: HarperCollins, 1996.*

Back It Up

Mickey Mantle was one of the most famous baseball players of all time. He was also one of the best. Yet even he had trouble dealing with pressure from his parents. Merlyn Mantle said her husband still felt pressure later in his career. Why do you think Mantle stopped wetting the bed? Write 200 words explaining why you think the pressure from Mantle's dad was so much greater than the pressure Mantle put on himself.

Mickey Mantle struggled with the pressures of youth sports before becoming a baseball star with the New York Yankees.

have private coaches or personal trainers. The parents might believe they are giving their children the best chance to succeed. But keeping up can be mentally difficult.

Sometimes there is greater motivation. Athletic scholarships can help great athletes pay for college. Some scholarships pay the entire bill. And a select few athletes even go on to professional sports careers. They make a living by playing the game. But achieving those things is incredibly difficult. Approximately 2 percent of high school athletes earn athletic scholarships. Even fewer go on to become professional athletes. And professional athletes in most sports make very little money. There is nothing wrong with working to achieve these goals. But experts warn that parents should not pressure their kids to do so. The end goals are so difficult that the pressure can backfire. Young athletes might work so hard they get hurt. Or the athletes might simply burn out and lose interest in playing.

Author Mark Hyman wrote of a well-known doctor he met in Los Angeles. The doctor was an orthopedic surgeon who operated on damaged elbows and shoulders of youth baseball pitchers.

"[The doctor] once told me of a recurring conversation he has with patients," Hyman wrote. "A young person confides that he does not want an operation and would prefer to quit his sport. But he's stuck. 'I don't know what to do because I don't want to disappoint my parents. It's so important to my dad.' "

Studies have shown that parents often have high goals for kids in sports. One study by Safe Kids Worldwide surveyed 752 paid and volunteer coaches. It found that many coaches feel pressure from parents to get an injured child back into a game. Approximately half of the 166 paid coaches reported that pressure. Approximately one-third of the 586 volunteer coaches said the same.

Supportive parents can help young athletes stay healthy as they participate in sports.

Youth sports coaches are supposed to put player safety over winning. But the Safe Kids Worldwide survey concluded that pressure from parents can make it hard for coaches to put safety first.

AVOIDING BURNOUT

Burnout is preventable. Experts say athletes, parents, and coaches should be aware of signs of burnout. Some of the signs are physical. An athlete might be tired all the time. This can lead to poor or inconsistent play.

One of the best ways to avoid burnout, experts say, is to ensure that all youth athletes have an offseason.

Burnout can also be seen in an athlete's mental state. The athlete might become irritable or even depressed. The athlete also might feel he or she is not valuable to the team. These symptoms are more common in athletes who tend to be perfectionists.

An athlete with burnout symptoms should cut back or take time off from the sport. Athletes can also try playing other sports rather than specializing in just one. This is especially true for younger athletes. In fact, the National Association for Sport and Physical Education says that specialization "poses more risks than rewards" for kids under 15.

Parents are especially important in preventing burnout. They should encourage positive thoughts about their child's role on the team. Parents should also listen to how their child is feeling about his or her sport. And most important, experts say, is parents should make sure young athletes have an offseason.

CHAPTER 4

A high school basketball coach yells orders to his players during a game.

BULLY COACHES

The Jaguars were 13 points down in the third quarter. The game was spinning out of control. The coach of the opposing team was not happy with the referees, and he was letting the referees know it.

Rhea Taylor was the basketball coach of the Jaguars at New Roads High School in Santa Monica, California. He felt all sportsmanship had been lost in the game. Taylor was having a hard time keeping his cool. He stood up and started to get animated. Then he caught himself and stopped.

"No. This isn't how we've been winning, and this isn't the style I've been using all year," Taylor thought. The Jaguars pulled it together and went on to win by seven points.

ESPN was at the Jaguars' game that day. The network was shooting footage for a piece on positive coaching for its *Outside the Lines* program. Taylor had formerly been a loud and critical coach on the sideline. He used bullying tactics to motivate his players. Bullying is an aggressive form of harassment. It occurs when one person intimidates a person in a weaker position. In sports, sometimes coaches try to motivate using fear, guilt, or intimidation. But there is growing evidence that those tactics can have negative results. So Taylor was working to change his behavior.

"You're doing this wrong and you're doing this wrong, and you are doing this wrong, and you need to do this better, and I don't like this about you and I don't like this about you and you need to change this," Taylor told ESPN, describing his former behavior.

But in the offseason, Taylor had watched a presentation by the PCA. The PCA stresses the magic ratio in coaching. The ratio is that coaches should make five supportive comments for every critical remark. PCA founder Jim Thompson developed this theory. His organization says kids perform better when coaches get close to the ratio.

Taylor thought the magic ratio was a great concept. "But I thought, how in the world am I possibly going to find five positives for every correction or criticism?" he said.

US women's national soccer team coach Pia Sundhage, *right*, jokes with forward Abby Wambach during a 2010 tournament.

Taylor decided he would stop screaming at his players. That season he tried a new, calmer coaching style. The Jaguars made it to the playoffs for the first time in five years. Then they won the first game. But the Jaguars fell behind early in the quarterfinals. Taylor felt himself going back to his old ways. But again he caught himself. Taylor stayed calm and positive. And the Jaguars got back in the game. They ended up barely losing in a close finish. Taylor said that his kids would never have gotten back into that game if had gone back to his ranting and raving coaching style.

"My kids would have crumbled from not only the pressure of the situation, but also the additional pressure I put on them," Taylor said.

WHAT DOES BULLYING LOOK LIKE?

There are a few clear signs of bullying by a coach, psychologist Dr. John Schinnerer said. They include a coach making an athlete feel that he or she is worthless. The coach might treat the athletes as if they are valued only by their performance. These criticisms can be relayed in many ways. Coaches might bully through words, body language, facial expression, or tone of voice. A coach can also bully by withdrawing support of an athlete. Bullying can lead to a chemical reaction in the brain. That can affect a kid's ability to think clearly, to learn, or to remember, a Penn State study showed. So for a coach who delivers his or her requests using intimidation and fear, an athlete might not remember any of what was said anyway.

STICKS AND STONES

Excelling in sports requires mental toughness. So some coaches believe that yelling at athletes can help toughen them up. However, studies have shown that is not the case.

Yelling and insulting kids can lead to lifelong problems. In the short term, these attacks can make kids feel bad about themselves. That can lead to anxiety. Over time, these verbal attacks can result in physical changes in kids' bodies. Verbal abuse can also affect kids' ability to think clearly, learn, or remember.

Silent abuse can also negatively affect kids. This can include acts such as intimidating players through facial expressions. Silent abuse can also simply be ignoring players. Coaches can insult players in more subtle ways, too. One seventh-grade basketball player remembered a subtle way in which his coach used to make players feel bad. The coach would split the players up into two teams.

"Then he said, 'OK, this group is the good players, and this group is the bad players,'" the player recalled. "That's just how he talked."

Some kids might not be fazed by comments like that. But those types of insults can become a big issue for others.

Dr. Joel Haber is a clinical psychologist. He said adults should be held responsible for bullying children involved in sports. According to Haber, "Bullying behavior is never acceptable, especially from the adults we trust to teach proper values and sportsmanship to our children."

KOOL-AID LEFT, KOOL-AID RIGHT

Kirk Zamora has long worked with the Hawks youth tackle football league in Duarte, California. He said youth coaching styles range from the military approach to the total opposite.

"There's the, 'Let's ask Johnny what he wants [approach],' and that's a disaster, too," Zamora said. "We have a coach that plays it in the middle, and his kids love him. He works with the six- to eight-year-olds,

SUPPORTING THE VOLUNTEER COACH

Steve Young was a top NFL quarterback during the 1990s. He led the San Francisco 49ers to victory in Super Bowl XXIX. And Young was named the Most Valuable Player. Young played for many coaches during his youth, college years, and 15 seasons in the NFL. But he believes that a child's very first coaches in sports have the most impact. Young says that children learn how to approach the game in their very first seasons. That is also when the kids learn to deal with adversity and how to adjust to new ideas. Young said, "So, I think my most influential coaches were my first couple, who were parent volunteers."

and he teaches and coaches. But at the end of it all, it's fun. His plays are [named] Kool-Aid Left, and Kool-Aid Right, and they win. Not all the time, but most of the time."

The Hawks have approximately 200 youth players from ages 6 to 14 years old. "It's okay to bark orders, but not to belittle a kid," said Zamora, who was a past president of the league. "And I've let a lot of these coaches go. You are dealing with a bully mentality, not only with the coaches but with the parents in the stands. It's widespread. They are verbally aggressive."

Zamora said his son played for a coach who was always critical. The coach made the kids on the team feel like they could not do anything right.

"The coach made them feel that way, and they didn't win," Zamora said. "But that coach left and another coach came in with a different style, and these same kids are winning."

WHAT CAN AN ATHLETE DO?

There is plenty written about how parents should deal with a bullying coach. But how should athletes deal with a coach who bullies or belittles them?

Dr. John Schinnerer is a psychologist. He said the first thing an athlete should do is listen to the feeling in their gut. Does the kid feel "angry, ashamed, guilty, anxious, or sad" when near the coach? If so, the kid should look for another coach.

A youth soccer coach gives directions to his players.

Changing coaches is often easier in a youth sports club or recreation league. The athlete can usually just go to another league or find another coach. But school teams are different. Switching schools is sometimes an option. But that is a much bigger decision than simply changing club teams.

Sometimes replacing an abusive coach is difficult. That can be the case if the abuse does not start until mid-season. Finding a willing and qualified replacement can be tricky. Many youth coaches are volunteers.

However, some leagues require coaches to be certified. That limits potential replacements. So teams are sometimes left with a dilemma. If they fire an abusive coach, the team might have to shut down. But abuse is never necessary. Athletes and their parents can leave the team at any time as well.

Regardless, the athlete needs to decide the best way to go forward. A coach who yells is not necessarily abusive. Sometimes a coaching style just does not motivate every athlete. In this case, the best course is for the athlete to share his or her concerns. Sometimes talking to the coach is the best bet. The coach might not realize his or her actions are having the wrong effect. Parents and teachers can also help an athlete and a coach better understand each other.

An abusive coach is another issue. Athletes should not be subject to abuse or bullying from coaches. Sharing these concerns with a coach can be a good first step. But coaches are authority figures. Sometimes they are hard to talk to. An athlete might fear getting kicked off the team or losing playing time for speaking up. In that case, athletes should go to their parents or school administrators.

Schinnerer said his own 10-year-old son was bullied by a swim coach. The coach was a woman in her mid-20s. Schinnerer said his son was told to shut up and that he was an embarrassment.

"He was yelled at and scolded in a tone of voice [that was disrespectful]," Schinnerer said. "He was told he would be punished for any mistakes he or his peers made in the future."

So Schinnerer spoke to the coach. The coach explained that she was trying to motivate her swimmers for the big meet the next day.

"She said that 9- and 10-year-old boys were 'squirrelly' and 'needed to be taken down a notch,' " Schinnerer recalled. "She was in full support of her coaches yelling at, embarrassing, and insulting young children to motivate them to swim faster. 'That's just the way swimming is,' she said."

Schinnerer and his son then left to find a new team.

ELEVEN RINGS

Some coaches believe in a militaristic approach. They believe that striking fear into athletes is motivating. Coaches have used these tactics for years. Yelling at and criticizing players is common.

Sometimes coaches yell simply to be heard. After all, sporting events can be loud. But yelling to be critical is different. This can be abusive. And sometimes this abuse makes a player think he or she is not good enough. All of this is the opposite of what Phil Jackson believes in.

A POSITIVE APPROACH

Rich Laski is a father of six children. He has served as a volunteer coach for five of his kids' sports teams, both boys and girls. Laski said he tries to use positive messages to motivate his athletes.

"This middle school age is a tough one," he said. "These kids are going through a lot—pimples, boys, hormones raging, and they are really insecure at that age. When I coached basketball, if a kid shot an air ball I would yell, 'That's OK, keep shooting.' If I yelled at him, 'Why did you take that shot?' I would lose that kid for the whole game."

Chicago Bulls coach Phil Jackson hugs Michael Jordan after they won the 1996 NBA title. It was their fourth of six together.

Jackson won two NBA championships as a player and 11 as a coach. No coach in league history has won more. Jackson believes in a positive approach to coaching. Positive coaching is not soft, he says. He says coaches do not have to be destructive or hurtful to look strong to their players. Instead, Jackson believes in balance. He tried to always keep his mood and actions steady through the ups and downs of a season. That is how he showed his players that he was strong.

When he first started coaching, Jackson would sometimes shout at his players. He took over as the Chicago Bulls' head coach in 1989. Shortly after, Jackson read about the magic ratio. The PCA, which developed the ratio, is focused more on high school age and younger. But Jackson said that the ratio is still effective at the professional level. Players at that level still question themselves sometimes. Jackson believes that compliments give the players confidence.

Jackson started balancing out positive remarks with critical ones. He soon led the Bulls to six NBA titles. Then he led the Los Angeles Lakers to five more. Derek Fisher played guard for the Lakers when Jackson coached the team. Fisher said of Jackson, "Even in games and also some of the practices where he would like to be [critical], because of the values of what he believes, in the terms of positive coaching, he'll hold back, he'll refrain."

CHAPTER 5

Former Penn State assistant football coach Jerry Sandusky was accused of systematic child abuse.

CHILD SEXUAL ABUSE IN SPORTS

Jerry Sandusky looked like the model citizen. He and his wife, Dottie, fostered and adopted children. He had a great job. For 32 years, he was an assistant football coach at Penn State University. That was a model program under head coach Joe Paterno. Also, Sandusky started a charity foundation to help kids. It was called The Second Mile.

However, Jerry Sandusky was not as he seemed. He was a child molester. He used his status and charity foundation to meet young children and sexually abuse them.

In 2008, a boy told his mother he was abused by Sandusky. The boy said the abuse started when he was younger and had attended Second

Mile camps. At first it seemed innocent. Sandusky would give the boy rides home from school and invite him to sleepovers at Sandusky's house. Sandusky gradually built up trust. As he did, the sexual abuse began. Sandusky was then a volunteer coach at the boy's school. Finally the boy spoke up. This began a major investigation of Sandusky by authorities.

On June 22, 2012, Sandusky was convicted of 45 counts of raping or fondling boys. The incidents included attacks on boys inside university buildings. The 68-year-old former coach was sent to prison. He is serving a 30- to 60-year term.

This news about Sandusky shocked many people. His abuse was widespread and calculated. More than 30 children have claimed that Sandusky sexually abused them. Even one of Sandusky's adopted sons was a victim.

Child abusers often build the trust of the child and the parents before starting the abuse. In many cases, coaches are treated like part of the family. This causes a child to be afraid to complain. Studies have shown that up to 70 percent of sexually abused children never talk about it. Mostly, the abused are too afraid or embarrassed to talk. But sometimes a child does not even understand what is happening to them.

In many sports, there is a natural closeness between the coach and athlete. It is both physical and emotional. Physical contact is often required for instruction and for safety. Emotional bonds can also form between athletes and coaches. Athletes have to trust their coaches. And in some cases that trust extends outside of the sport. Coaches spend long hours with their athletes. They travel together. Sometimes coaches even act in parental ways for their athletes.

In one case, a promising gymnast said he trained with a coach for four years before sexual abuse began. By then, the athlete was eight years old. His family was very close with the coach. The athlete later said he was embarrassed and blamed himself. He thought he must have done something to cause the sexual abuse. By the time he was 12, the athlete tried to stand up to the coach. But the coach warned that he would stop coaching the athlete if he told his parents.

THE NUMBERS

One in every four girls and one in every six boys is sexually abused before the age of 18. And studies have shown that some are 10 years old or younger when the abuse starts. Approximately 12 percent of sexually abused females and 28 percent of sexually abused males are that young.

Those numbers are alarming. However, researchers are encouraged by reports that child sexual abuse has declined dramatically. According to a story in the *New York Times*, cases of child sexual abuse

WHAT IS SEXUAL ABUSE?

Sexual abuse in sports includes all sexual touching between an adult and a child under the age of 18. It can also include sexual touching between children when there is an age, development, or size difference. But sexual abuse can also occur without any touching. It is sexual abuse when a child is encouraged to look at sexual images, watch sexual activities, or behave in sexually inappropriate ways. Sexual abuse can involve the use or threat of force to make a child take part in sexual activities. The abuser is usually a person known to the child. In sports that person can be someone such as a coach, teammate, or staff member.

Victims of sexual abuse are often reluctant to come forward.

in the United States decreased by more than 60 percent from 1992 to 2010. Dr. David Finkelhor is the director of the Crimes Against Children Research Center at the University of New Hampshire. He found that more children who are victims of sexual abuse are reporting it. He cites, in part, a greater public awareness of sexual abuse for the encouraging numbers in recent years.

Overall, though, experts say it is difficult to tell how widespread child sexual abuse is. That is because only 10 to 20 percent of cases are reported. The Centers for Disease Control and Prevention (CDC) said this is because sexual abuse is often hidden. Victims feel panic, shame, and disbelief associated with the act.

Chris Gavagan knows that feeling of shame all too well. At 14, he fell victim to a coach who sexually abused him for three years. It took 15 years before Gavagan told anybody about the abuse. Instead, his behavior changed and he became an angry kid. He described the experience in a television interview:

> *There was a man with the worst intentions, with a smiling face, who gained the trust of everyone around him, and he used me in any way that he needed to for his own purposes while saying that everything was for my best. . . . I was raised by two of the greatest parents any boy could ever hope for, who did everything to teach me right and*

wrong, and then the moment I was out from under their watchful eye, someone came along and undermined, in incremental ways, every day everything they had taught of right and wrong.

Gavagan directed a documentary called *Coached into Silence*. It analyzed sexual abuse of male athletes by male coaches. Gavagan said he was afraid to let his friends know about the abuse. He thought they would think less of him. Eventually he told them, though. And when he did, they all had the same question: *Why didn't you tell me?*

"I spent so many years thinking that nobody could love me," Gavagan said. "The support that I thought was never there, was there all along. If I had just found a way to tell the truth to the people who cared about me. If I had told them while the abuse was ongoing. Not only would I have stopped the abuse in its tracks, but I would have been able to fully experience the loving relationships I was surrounded by."

Experts say it is common for victims of sexual abuse to blame themselves. And doing so can lead to depression and many other emotional problems. The immediate

CHECKING IT OUT

Many sports leagues and organizations require criminal background checks on adults who work with children. This is meant to be an effective safety measure. These checks are not always perfect, though. Some background check companies only search in the applicant's home state. Another problem is that most sexual abuse is unreported. That means an abuser's past might not show up on a background check. In addition, some nonprofit organizations only screen volunteers. They do not screen for anyone earning a salary or a small amount of money. On top of all of that, background checks can be expensive. Still, experts suggest background checks be done on everyone over the age of 17 who works around or with children.

effects sexual abuse can have on a child include behavioral changes or problems in school. Some people develop eating disorders. Other responses can include headaches, difficulty sleeping, scratching until bleeding, and major weight loss or gain.

WARNING SIGNS

There is no one sign to help a parent recognize a child sexual abuser. But if a number of factors are present, parents should be concerned.

"If there's an adult coach who spends more time with children than he does with adults, who wants to be with your child more than you do, and creates access and one-on-one opportunities to do so, that's a major warning sign," Gavagan said. "If a coach is always volunteering to give your child a ride to and from practice or giving him gifts or taking him out for meals or texting him, that's a major warning sign."

Other warning signs include an adult coach discussing inappropriate topics with a child. Unwanted physical contact can be a warning sign, too. This can include things such as hugging, touching, kissing, tickling, or wrestling. Even holding a child when the child does not want to be held can be a warning sign.

REACHING OUT

The USOC launched a yearlong campaign in April 2013 called Make the Commitment: Stop Abuse in Sport. The goal of this program is to inform and educate children, coaches, parents, and sports personnel about child

STRAIGHT TO THE SOURCE

The Grooming Process

According to the USOC's SafeSport program, child sexual abusers use a systematic process called grooming to prey on and eventually control their victims. The process has six steps. The first four steps come before sexualizing the relationship:

1. Targeting the victim – An offender will identify a child and determine his or her vulnerabilities.
2. Gaining trust – Through watching and gathering information about the child, an offender will become acquainted with a child's needs.
3. Filling a need – Offenders will often lavish gifts, extra attention, and affection to forge a bond with their victims.
4. Isolating the child – By developing a special relationship with the child, an offender creates situations in which [he] or she is alone with the child.

Source: "Child Sexual Abuse." SafeSport. *SafeSport, 2013. Web. 8 Aug. 2013.*

Consider Your Audience

You just read the SafeSport program's process for how a child sexual abuser plots his crimes. It is sensitive material and difficult to read about. Consider that you are asked to talk with a group of young children to educate them about appropriate and inappropriate behavior of adults. What part of this information would you use in your talk? How would you rewrite this to make it more child sensitive?

Experts warn that parents should look out for adults who show too much physical affection toward youths.

sexual abuse at all levels. The program provides education and training from experts in child sexual abuse. The outreach is under the umbrella of the USOC's ongoing SafeSport program.

US judoka Kayla Harrison overcame sexual abuse to become an Olympic champion in 2012.

On the surface, the USOC campaign appears to be similar to many other outreach programs. But this campaign goes deeper. One of its major goals is to make all children aware of what is inappropriate behavior by an adult. The campaign Web site has a tab titled "For Athletes." There is a link there to a page called "Know What's Okay." This lists questions and answers to potentially real situations. There is another link that tells athletes where and how to get help for sexual child abuse. Under

"Find Support," the information reads like a letter written directly to the reader:

> *You may be here because you have seen or experienced certain things and you aren't sure what to do next. . . . When you feel comfortable sharing your feelings, there are confidential resources available to help. It's important that you share this information with people who can help you and protect others. Therapists, experts, and organizations can provide the answers and support you. If you want to report an issue or reach out to an expert, we can point you in the right direction.*

Under the "Counseling" link, there is a crisis phone number. The Web site also includes contact information for the USOC's senior sports psychologist.

Many experts stress the importance of a sexually abused child having someone to reach out to who will not judge the situation. Having a person to reach out to is a main way a child can stop sexual abuse and get help.

OVERCOMING ABUSE

Kayla Harrison won the United States' first gold medal in judo at the 2012 London Olympic Games. The accomplishment was far more than an athletic victory. Harrison was 22 years old when she won. As a teenager, Harrison was at the top of her sport. But her coach was sexually abusing her at the same time. At 16, Harrison finally told someone. The coach was eventually sentenced to prison. But the experience left Harrison wanting to give up on everything, including judo. Her mother did not let her, though. Harrison began working with a new coach, Jimmy Pedro. He and his staff helped her work through her emotions. They also helped her become an Olympic champion. "[The sexual abuse] was definitely the hardest thing that I've ever had to overcome," Harrison said. "I couldn't have done it without [my coaches] and without my family supporting me."

With support from parents, coaches, and teammates, youth sports can be a positive, growing experience.

Gavagan lived through years of painful silence. He knows how important it is to take that step. He urges sexual abuse victims to speak up.

"The support system is there," he says. " If you're being abused, there is no time like the present to tell somebody that you trust and you can begin to heal and go on with your life."

Kids deal with a variety of pressures and issues in sports. No two issues are exactly the same. But no matter what, there are places a kid can go for help. Sometimes that means going to a parent, coach, teacher, administrator, or friend. If there is no one close who is available to help, kids can also find resources online. These Web sites can help kids find solutions to the issues or connect them with people who can help.

LADY
23
DEMONS

DISCUSSION QUESTIONS

Another View

In Chapter Three, a study of 340 parents at children's soccer games revealed more than half of the parents were angry at some point while watching their children's match. The parents were mostly mad at referees, their own child's play, and their child's team. List five tips to help parents stay positive while watching their children participate in sports.

Dig Deeper

Chapter Two discusses how overtraining can lead to a child's physical and mental burnout in a sport. Have you ever felt burnout from sports? If not, have you ever noticed burnout symptoms in a friend? If so, write a few paragraphs explaining what caused the burnout and how it could be prevented in the future.

Say What?

In Chapter Five, Chris Gavagan, who was sexually abused by a coach beginning at age 14, lists warning signs that may indicate to parents that a coach is a sexual predator. Pretend you have been asked to give a talk to kids your age about sexual abuse. Write a list of warning signs that kids and parents should be aware of.

GLOSSARY

adversity
A state or situation of serious difficulty.

anxiety
A fearful concern or uneasiness.

conditioning
The process of training to become physically fit through a routine of exercise, diet, and rest.

demeaning
To make a person or thing seem of little importance or value.

hazing
Playing unpleasant tricks on someone or forcing that person to do unpleasant things in order for that person to join a club or group.

hydration
To supply the body with necessary fluid or moisture.

militaristic
The use of military methods such as discipline and force to gain power and achieve goals.

scholarship
Money that is given to a student by a school or organization to help pay for the student's education.

viral
When something spreads rapidly, such as a video on the internet.

volunteer
A person who does work without getting paid for it.

FOR MORE INFORMATION

SELECTED BIBLIOGRAPHY

"Counseling." *TeamUSA.org*. United States Olympic Committee, 2013. Web. 8 Aug. 2013.

De Lench, Brooke C. *Home Team Advantage: The Critical Role of Mothers In Youth Sports*. New York: Collins, 2006. Print.

Hyman, Mark. *Until It Hurts: America's Obsession with Youth Sports and How It Harms Our Kids*. Boston, MA: Beacon, 2009. Print.

FURTHER READINGS

Bigelow, Bob, and Tom Moroney, and Linda Hall. *Just Let the Kids Play: How to Stop Other Adults from Ruining Your Child's Fun and Success in Youth Sports*. Deerfield Beach, FL: Health Communications, 2001. Print.

Engh, Fred. *Why Johnny Hates Sports*. Garden City Park, NY: Square One, 2002. Print.

Fiorino, Tony. *Kids In Sports: A Tactical Guide for Parents and Coaches*. Somers, NY: Intrinsic Partners LLC, 2009. Print.

WEB SITES

To learn more about high-pressure youth sports, visit ABDO Publishing Company online at **www.abdopublishing.com**. Web sites about high-pressure youth sports are featured on our Book Links page. These links are routinely monitored and updated to provide the most current information available.

PLACES TO VISIT

Newport Sports Museum
100 Newport Center Drive #100
Newport Beach, CA 92660
949-721-9333
www.newportsportsmuseum.org
This museum aims to promote healthy lifestyles through its memorabilia and partnerships with famous athletes. In addition, the museum has free programs meant to help instill confidence in children and teens.

US Olympic Training Center
1 Olympic Plaza
Colorado Springs, CO 80909
719-866-4618
www.teamusa.org
The Colorado Springs Olympic Training Center contains top-end training facilities for US Olympic hopefuls. Many athletes live and train here year-round. A 45-minute tour is available to the public.

INDEX

ABOUT THE AUTHOR

Maryann Hudson has written three books about sports and sports issues. As an investigative sports reporter for the *Los Angeles Times*, she won numerous national and regional awards. Hudson is a graduate of the University of Southern California's School of Journalism. She is currently a freelance writer and lives with her family in Pasadena, California.